Can Panda Get It?

Written by Sheryl Webster
Illustrated by Sally Garland

Run up the hill to get it, Panda!

It fell into the mud!
Puff!
Huff!
Huff!
Puff!

I am sad.
I can tug it!

Tug!
Tug!
Blap!

Go up and get it!
Sob!
Sob!

Panic not! I can get it!

I can kick it off!
Biff!
Baff!
Help!
Boff!

Kiss!
Pop!
Hiss!